I Am Not An Island

Elizabeth Lane
I Am Not An Island

In memory of my grandad

I Am Not An Island
ISBN 978 1 76041 585 3
Copyright © Elizabeth Lane 2018

First published 2018 by
GINNINDERRA PRESS
PO Box 3461 Port Adelaide 5015
www.ginninderrapress.com.au

Contents

Being Frank	7
What is the Colour of Love?	8
Expecting	9
Mouthy Madam	10
Mummy's Running Commentary	11
The teeny weeny pink bikini	12
When My Child Looks at Me With Murder in Her Eyes	14
A Daughter's Response	16
Young Mother	17
Childhood Embarrassment	18
Based on a true story	21
Dad's Car	24
Stepdad	25
Portrait of Artist's Father	26
Dodge	28
Misogynist	29
Hope I Once Held	30
Travelling Through the Dark	31
What My Mother Taught Me	32
Filling the Void	33
A Sad Story With a Happy Ending	35
Margit	36
Maternal Monarch	38
Respect	39
Willie Wagtail	40
'The Frog and the Badger'	41
Half-sisters	42
The Oldest Teenager in Adelaide	43
The Invisible Ties	44
Past Offences	45
Sunday Dinner	46
Insular	47

George and John	49
Be brave	52
Back to the Future	53
Avatar of the Amazon	54
Olives and Wine	55
Missionaries	56
Uncle	57
Termites	58
Dream home	59
Wedding	60
Cake Topper	62
Ode to Matrimony	63
This is Just to Say	64
The Extension	65
The Erosion	66
The Jar	67
Goodbye Black Dog	68
Franz Marc	69
Disappointment Man	70
Big Men	71
Checking In	73
The End of the Love Affair I Had With the Thought of You	74
Attention Seeking	75
Brief Encounter	76
Grief and Loss	77
Shadow Play	78
Discourse	79
Sylvia	80
Runaway Idea	82
Dusted with Icing Sugar	83
Is This Love?	84
The Train	85
Heart Forms	86
The World	87

Being Frank

If you don't have anything nice to say
say nothing
unless it will make people laugh
then it must be said.
Don't be a full sack
or an empty one with a hole in it
because you can't put or keep anything
in either of them.
Always tell people when you have no bananas.
If it rains expect your feet to get wet
but always keep them firmly fixed on the ground.
The truth must always be offered
when an opinion is asked for.
People should not get too big for their boots
and should be informed when they are doing so.
Optimism is just a nice word for being delusional.
Reality is harsh and disappointing
but if you don't get your hopes up
you shouldn't end up too disappointed.

What is the Colour of Love?

Is love red
like the blood that pumps
through my veins?
Or is love blue
like the depths of the ocean
where my options are sink or swim?
Maybe love is green
like budding leaves
that grow on trees in springtime.
Perhaps love is yellow
like butter melting
on warm toast.
If love were orange
it would fill the sky
as the sun went down.
Love in purple
is like bruised skin
both bold and fragile.
But love is a spectrum
it is all colours
and it is in all things.

Expecting

Unplanned and unprepared for the journey,
confirmation came in the passing of water
in a tiny white vessel.
Sailing a sea of thoughts
the swaying made her sick.
An unknown destination in clear sight
unlike any place she'd ever been,
both beautiful and confronting.

Mouthy Madam

My bossy toddler
push and shove.
She is a force
of lips, teeth and tongue.
I have met my match.
Animated articulation
spirited wit
fervent response.
She stares me down
with eyes of still water blue
and steps upon her soapbox.
Her tiny moon face
glowing and luminous
seriously set
to deliver her rebuttal.
She has been sent
to challenge me
test my strength
my patience.
And teach me another kind of truth.

Mummy's Running Commentary

Can you wipe my bum?
Can you turn on the tap?
I am hungry.
I want something to eat.
I want a kiwi fruit.
I want cornflakes.
Can I have something to eat?
Where are we going today?
Can we go to the shops?
What's that?
Who is that?
What is their name?
I want to go home.
Can we go home?
Can I watch TV?
Can you turn it on?
I don't want to watch this anymore.
I want to go outside.
Can you open the door?
Now can I have a kiwi fruit?
Can I have a lollipop?
Excuse me mummy,
Please?

The teeny weeny pink bikini

You are a picture of perfection
svelte, lean and statuesque
you are
shining example
of what society tells women
to aspire to
unmarked
smooth
sleek
youthful.
A suntanned deity.
But to me you are still
that teeny weeny, pink baby
chubby, roly-poly arms and legs
I still see the cuddly, squishy, squirmy
little bundle.
I don't want to let you go.
If I do let you go out into the world
the sun kissed goddess you have become
in that teeny weeny pink bikini
I am scared that I have lost you.
They will lure you
they will stroke you
preen you and whisper in your ear.

But they will maul you, grab, claw
and paw at you
and when they have had they're fun
they will toss you aside
for the next, newer, younger, prettier, picture of perfection
so please don't go out in that teeny weeny pink bikini
stay here with me
and be my teeny weeny pink baby forever.

When My Child Looks at Me With Murder in Her Eyes

Ice-blue eyes
narrow
focusing in
on the target
– me
like a laser beam
like a sniper.
Those eyes of steel
like the wind
in a storm.
The lightning-bolt look
that pierces me
paralyses, stuns
cuts me down to size.
If those eyes
and that glare
were any sharper
I would be sliced dead
instantly.
Those probing eyes
that have been able
to see inside of me
from the day you were born
have the power to
both comfort
and cut me
caress me
and burn me.

Eyes like a dream
and a nightmare.
Who sees who?
Who is watching over who?
Are you my verity?
Or am I yours?

A Daughter's Response

I watched her do it
one year in five
my mother
has dug in for a repeat performance
I carry the memory of her happy
a spinning top
a wind-up toy
and I think
I should offer my mother words
that she can hold in her hands
as comfort
as a reminder
that she is not a monster
she is not a suicide doll
I don't want her lifeless
a souvenir
I want her alive
and alive and alive
forever alive

Young Mother

I am irresponsible.
I must be easy or promiscuous
ignorant and careless
or selfish and manipulative.
I did it for the money.
But yet I must sacrifice
dreams and aspirations.
Do they have the same dad?
Is the father around?
Are you married?
Do you support yourself?
Are you receiving benefits?
Is it any of your business?
I must be clean and tidy,
cleanliness and tidiness must be a top priority.
Food preparation must always be considered.
Everyday must revolve around meal times
and what I will be feeding my children.
My every waking minute must be consumed by them.
But I am irresponsible.

Childhood Embarrassment

As always
at the end of the school year
our class would have a party
and all the students must bring
a plate of food to school to share.
As my mum was not
a big one for baking
or cooking
or preparing food in general
my offerings were always pretty boring
and slapped together
at the last minute.
But this particular year
Grade two
was outright humiliating.
My mum used to occasionally
pack me for lunch
a baked bean sandwich.
I hated baked beans.
But in a sandwich
I loathed them even more.

The bread would soak up
the baked bean slop
and end up soggy
and bright orange
and any attempt
to eat the thing
would result in the sandwich
falling apart
and I would end up
covered in orange baked bean stains.
So for my grade two end of year class party
my mum decided
to send me to school
with a plateful
of soggy, cold baked bean sandwiches.
My classmates had brought cake, iced Vovos, chips
fairy bread and party pies.
Nice, normal party food
and I had baked bean and bread slop.
I put the plate on the table
quickly and quietly
before anyone saw me
and then spent the rest of the day
pretending me and my plate
didn't know each other.

From a distance
I watched my plate's interactions.
No one was approaching
no one was eating
except one
freckle-faced
curly-haired boy
who gobbled them up.
I felt sorry for the person
who had to sit next to him
for the rest of the day,
they would be having a smelly afternoon.
But at least I wouldn't be taking
the baked bean slop home again
and run the risk
of my mum making me eat them for dinner.

Based on a true story

Seeing things through one eye
complete acts unseen
memories scrubbed out
a vignette snapshot
edges gradually fading away
into non-existence
'No, that never happened,
that's not how it was!'
Maybe it's all about perspective
where you were standing
when it all went down…
…but it feels like
from where I am standing,
reviewing the stored footage
from my hard drive,
you have left a lot on the cutting room floor
edited scenes and scenarios
heavy-handedly
so the lighting is definitely in your favour.
I do not like your 'director's cut'
it leaves almost a whole era
reduced down to a small passage of time
the memories have been spread too thin
not enough butter on 'my' toast!
I am left
in the shadows
looking like the villain
the antagonist.
Selective memory?
Repressed memories?

Dementia or Alzheimer's maybe?
You would definitely and defiantly disagree.
'Accurate recollection' you'd call it.
'I remember'
…but I was there too
and although I will openly admit
my memory does not always show up
on time
but I am certain
you are leaving much of the facts out
and definitely and defiantly placing yourself in the rosy frame
and me in the dog house
You lack a complete recollection
of said time frame
it could be argued, by me,
but I won't
because it is an argument I will not win…

…BUT if I were going to attempt it
I would argue
the reason your memories
are so patchy
so sparse
is because during said time frame
you were not actually there
unavailable
absent
detached
and so in your account of a 'true story'
my character is two-dimensional
large parts of me
and my past
missing
but that's OK with you
because in your version
you are always the hero.

Dad's Car

A giant rubbish-eating,
guzzling monster.
It collects more food wrappers
than our household bin.
Bottles, cans, copper wire.
Tupperware growing mould,
it smells like damp dirty socks.
Suspension so rough
it squeaks
it bounces
passengers feel seasick
at the end of long journeys.
The children sit
with knees under chins
because all foot space is packed
with flotsam and jetsam.
It is the Bermuda triangle
items enter
never to be seen again.
Jackets, jumpers, T-shirts
even a remote control.
It is a junkyard
on four wheels.

Stepdad

I close my eyes
and a timeline of your faces
morphs through the years
of your existence.
Infant, child, teenager
you as a young man
I do not know you
until
the face appears
of you at the age
we met.
The faces represent
the eras of you
including when we coexisted
but why now
after you have left,
first emotionally
and then physically
and then you left this earth altogether
why are you showing yourself to me?
What could you want from me now?

Portrait of Artist's Father

Shadow cast across the side of your face
tricoloured beard
white grey and black
warm pink and apricot shades
make up the patchwork of your skin.
Lines around the eyes
the stories of your life
the years of your existence.
Black jacket
white shirt
tiny flash of red from your tie.
Hands with purple
knuckles protruding
a golden ring.
Looking down
you are thoughtful
lost in those thoughts.
What colour are your eyes?
They look dark
almost black
but that could be
the shadows
and the play of light
that are hiding their true hue.
Sat in a chair
Is that a walking stick
under your hand?
Do you have a limp?
An injury from war?
Can you see into the future?

Do you know?
Your son will go to war
and die?
And that is why
you look so melancholy.

Dodge

You are every man
that has ever rejected me;
told me I'm not good enough
I'm unlovable.
I seek out male attention
because of you
in an attempt
to bandage over
the gaping wounds
you left me with
when you abandoned me.
The aching pain
of wanting.
The squeeze
and the pull
of intense desire,
the desire to be
wanted
accepted
loved
was created the day you turned your back on me.

Misogynist

The loathsome beast
foul and repellent
emerges
from out of the bog,
barely evolved
past a single celled organism.
Your presence
upon the sensitive and compassionate,
the insightful and understanding
is destructive.
Imposing your offensive
pollution,
pillaging and plundering
faith and love.
Raping spirits
and leaving souls
damaged and devoid
go creature
return to the dark hole
from which you crawled out of.

Hope I Once Held

Buried deep in the pit
of my gut
is the hope
I once held
that I would be
engulfed by you,
I would float
in the warm golden liquid
of your love.
Comforted, soothed
and pacified
by that strong and silent
centre of you.

Travelling Through the Dark

Travelling through the dark I came across a fox
standing on the edge of Nangkita Road
she was leading her two pups across.
I braked hard and sat idling.
By the glow of high beams I watched them
one pup fled left into the shadows
the other sat in the middle of the road.
The mother's eyes darting from me to them.
My fingers wrapped around the steering wheel
my foot down hard on the brake
I thought about my neighbours
what they would say if they knew I'd stopped.
My car aimed for home
engine purring steadily under the hood
I waited while the family passed
probably aimed for home themselves.
I thought hard for all of us – my stopping
– saved these killers' lives.

What My Mother Taught Me

Independence
to care about human rights
and human suffering.
Love animals.
Follow my heart.
Be creative.
Money isn't everything
and we can make do with what we've got.
Words and books are important
and enrich our lives
and deserve great respect.
Stand up for what you believe in
and give a voice
to those who aren't heard.
Family is most important
always be there for them
when they need you.
Be helpful.
Care for others.
And work hard.

Filling the Void

She grew up
always
knowing who she was.
She knew what was important
and she knew how
she should be living life.
But there was a void
a piece of her heart missing
and without a complete heart
how could she ever truly love herself?
She tried to fill the hole with the love
and adoration of men
but it never worked.
That love and admiration never fit
inside the void.
The void could only be filled
by the love and attention of one man
Daddy
But that was something she was never going to get
and even if he did decide
to offer it to her
it could never fill the void
for the little girl that lived inside her.
So one day she decided
that the void was a part of her
just like her eyes
and her toes
and her laugh.

And so instead of trying to fill the void
with substitutes
she would let the void be what it was
and she would love it for what it was
a void
a part of her
a contributor to who she was
and a reminder
of how important the love of family is.

A Sad Story With a Happy Ending

Once upon a time
there was a brown dog
full of joy
full of love.
On the darkest days
the brown dog would grin
and bring cheer to all he met.
Then one night
that brown dog
went on an adventure.
In solid dark
he silently crept off
through loose fence paling
and unknowing
walked out onto a road
straight into headlights
and had the life knocked out of him.
Broken smiles
shattered hearts
an ocean of tears
and a terrible gaping void.
The brown dog was dead
never to return.
But…
28 days later
the golden dog
who was the brown dog's mate
gave birth
to 8 sons and 3 daughters.

Margit

Cocooned in waves of white cotton
Propped up
And positioned
By overinflated pillows
You slept
Mouth open
Wisps of hair floating
Reaching for the ceiling.
You looked small
Lost
Misplaced
But you sensed my presence
And woke.
As soon as we locked eyes
I knew
You were still you
The sparkle in your eye
Was where is should be
And you smiled
And my worries
Pain, grief and hopelessness
Began to melt.
I sat at the foot of your bed
and inhaled your words
Like a greedy infant
Consuming it's mother's milk.
You grounded me
Settled me
Reminded me of who I am
And where I come from.

And from your hospital bed
You kissed me better
And sent me on my way.

Maternal Monarch

Floating colour
orange and black
flashes.
Mini amber lights
signalling
to me
remember where you come from
remember joy
remember dance
remember smile.
We are one
we are connected.
Tiny paper puppets on string
flitting across a green backdrop.
Sucking up the nectar
enjoying the sun
after transformation
and a restricted universe
to start a new life
of freedom
of lightness
of peace.

Respect

In my world
You are king
A symbol
Of honesty
Dependability
And giving.
In the big world
You are a man
An everyday man
Working-class
Blending in
Head down.
In your world
You are living
Your life
A simple existence
Doing your bit
Helping yours
hurting no one.
But in my world
You are king.

Willie Wagtail

Patchwork black and white and grey
but your spirit is a rainbow
a flying totem
of the paternal past
a reminder
of my heritage
my lineage
loss, grief and discoveries
connection
meaning
understanding.
Willie wagtail
you tell a story of all times
from all over this land
but you also tell me
a personal story
a story of
my past.

'The Frog and the Badger'

Once were allies
A place of understanding
And protection
From the harsh world.
When there was nothing
And no one
They had each other
Always.
But now they are lost
And alone
Badger lost frog to betrayal and lies
And an unknown evil
And frog lost badger
To anger and intolerance.
Childhood confidants
Siblings
True brothers
Gone
And their hearts are broken.

Half-sisters

I embarrassed you
you let me down.
You said martyr
I said self-centred.
You walked away
I stormed out.
We both avoided
facing each other.
Opposing perspectives
conflicting expectations
drove a wedge
splitting us further apart.
Maybe that half-bloodline
makes us so different
divides us.
Two weeks passed
anger subsided
emptiness took its place
so I came to you.
Because without you
I don't feel whole.

The Oldest Teenager in Adelaide

Refuse to grow up
take responsibility
act your age
behave sensibly
and mature.
Risky behaviour
and a lack of self-awareness
and understanding of consequences.
It is time,
accept the ageing process
and the fact that you are not a kid any more.
If your teens were your glory years
then you future must seem pretty bleak
because those years are gone
you can't keep clinging
and trying to relive them
in a hope of willing that time
back into existence.
Let go.
Grow up
and start appreciating
life for the now.

The Invisible Ties

Our souls are linked
in this time
and eternity
we have known each other
in all our forms
dimensions
and lifetimes
we are kindred spirits
you and I
not just kin
not just cousins
even more than brother and sister.
We travel together
and apart
but we are always able
to locate the other
when we are separated.
Our pasts are intertwined
and will continue to
weave a web
that holds us together
into the future and forever.
Time will pass
and we will not see each other
until we land in the same place
at the same time
and we are exactly the same
to each other
as always.

Past Offences

Why is it necessary to remind me
of the mistakes I've made
I don't forget
I can't forget
guilt won't let me
but I have tried to forgive myself
I can't change them
undo, erase
they are embedded in the foundations
of my past
they are set firmly
in the person I was
but I will always carry them around with me.
Do you feel the need to remind me
that I am not really a good person
or the person I want to be?
Strive to be.
Does it make you feel better about yourself?
Ease some of your guilt?
By pointing out my wrong doing
if your aim is to make me feel
small, worthless and that my efforts are pointless
then job well done.

Sunday Dinner

Mother starts to lay the table
laying tablecloth
of leaves and vines.
I know by this single act
we are having a visitor
for dinner.
Mother never uses that tablecloth
for just us.
Dad, my brothers and I
not important enough
for the best tablecloth.
It can't be Grandma and Grandpa either.
The special guest
must be more important still.
Mother irons out the creases with her hand
carefully and lovingly
trying her hardest
not to hurt the poor thing.
Mother sets the table
with our best crockery and cutlery
unaware of my presence
oblivious to the fact that I am spying,
watching every move she makes
in the hope that she might give me a clue
of who we are to expect.
Mother straightens the knives
scans the table one last time
and turns and looks at me
'Love, go and put on your Sunday best.'

Insular

You are self-absorbed
self-obsessed
and self-centred.
All about you
what you've got
where you've been.
You measure a person's worth
by the size of their pay cheque
and whether they own a house
not by the contents of their character
their ability to show compassion
or whether they live a thoughtful
and giving life.
You live in a world
that revolves only
around you
your possessions
your achievements
and your desires.

But while you are so wrapped up
in your little world
walking around with blinkers on
you miss out
on helping
those in need
you miss out on true beauty
that lives in the simple things
you miss out on meeting
the unusual
the creative
the visionary.
In your selfish little world
you live an ordinary life.

George and John

I remember the night the call came through
Mum bundled us into the car
in our pyjamas and dressing gowns
half asleep.
I stared at the black night sky
and watched the stars sparkle
while I thought about what Mum had told us.
We got to Gran and Grandad's
their faces long and grey
blank expressions
but the pain buried deep in their eyes
spoke of a depth of emotion that I had not yet encountered
in my short life.
It was my first funeral
I had never seen so many people wearing black.
The scene was from a silent movie
all the characters with the colour drained out of them
like zombies
wandering blind and numb.
The huge ornate Greek Orthodox church
was full
an indication of all the hearts
you had both touched.
The priest came down the isle
singing and chanting
swinging a chamber
that billowed out smoke
in words and tradition
that were completely foreign to me.

I sat surrounded by family
yet separated from those closest to me.
I tried to make sense of it all.
The priest spoke
I didn't understand.
My uncle turned and looked at me
an expression of such utter sorrow
like I had never seen on him
I didn't understand.
When the service finished
people formed a line
making their way to the front of the church
to the tiny white coffin.
I joined the queue
and when I reached the front
I looked in
and there you both were
nestled in
face to face
eyes shut
but you were grey
lifeless
not as I remembered
I didn't understand.

I felt sick
lost
scared and confused.
The little white boat-shaped coffin
was lowered into the ground
I wanted someone to explain
help me understand
why this was happening
why my cousins were gone
when they were only little boys?
But no one could explain
because they didn't understand either.
So I said goodbye
and promised to never forget you.
I am an adult now
but you both have always been in my heart
forever my cousins
forever children.

Be brave

Be brave
With your love
Never afraid
Never ashamed
You are the sun
And I am the moon
In our little world
Believe
In this
A bond
Built
From twigs
And twine
Our nest
We built
Together
Forget not
This love
No matter
What unsettles
Upsets and disturbs
Nothing
Will break it
Your love
This love
Our love

Back to the Future

I crawled in
and took my seat
while the other three waited.
In the ignition
key was inserted
turned
and the engine
whirred and screamed
to life
then a low rumble.
The gears were pushed into place
and we began to roll
every bump was felt
a bang
a clang.
I looked behind
to see what had fallen off
but there was nothing.
The engine whined
the pitch heightening
as the car sped up
a hiss
and then a kick back
and the gear was changed.
I thought we had snapped through time
crossed over
the space time continuum
but we hadn't.
We were still on the freeway
in 2015.

Avatar of the Amazon

A graphic representation
of the alter ego
with weapons
and crescent shield
a high helmet of hair
and one long sparkling earring.
The Avatar of the Amazon
does her circular dance
posturing and posing
a manifestation
of a Greek goddess
an icon
a reconstructed character
to represent her digital persona.
Embodying
a statuesque and muscular
warrior woman
worthy of adoration
and reverence.
Through battle
fighting resistance
building strength
she hunts down her enemies
and destroys them.
But underneath
the rippling and bulging
muscular physique
is the gentle heart
of an Earth Mother.

Olives and Wine

Green olives float
in a pool of golden oil.
Blood-red wine sloshes
in crystal glasses.
Olives to lips
sips of merlot.
Flushed cheeks
glassy eyes.
Green olives stuffed
with salty anchovies.
Blood-red wine blots
the crisp white tablecloth.
Olives to lips
sips of merlot.
Jovial laughter
warm humming chatter.
Green olives marinated
in fragrant herbs.
Blood-red wine stains
on teeth.
Olives to lips
sips of merlot.
Voices raised
heated disagreements.
Green olives eaten.
Blood-red wine drunk.
Oil is unoccupied.
Glasses are empty.
The dining room is in disarray.
To be dealt with tomorrow.

Missionaries

(the jungle speaks)

Jungle creatures watched
as the family
hustled back and forth.
Pastel belongings bursting
and overflowing
from cardboard boxes.
Clouds of smoke
carried by winds
took away remnants of families' aromas.
The watching animals
could sense the adults sadness
and smell the children's fear.

Uncle

'It's not supposed to look like this,'
Uncle said.
'The sides are all wrong,
the roof isn't straight
and it leaks water.
I think the problem is,'
he continued
'the foundation is lopsided
and if the foundation isn't straight
the whole structure
is out,
cockeyed
crooked
doesn't sit flush.'
Uncle pointed out,
'The slab
that you are building your future on
needs to be right
strong and straight.
There is little room for mistakes
when it comes to the base.
All other aspects of the structure are affected
they take their cues from the foundation,'
concluded Uncle.

Termites

Pointed skyscrapers
built from mud and excrement.
Grey dusty towers.
A porous fortress.
The mounds inhabitants remain within
gathered in galleries
making the most of the moving sun.
Tiny white herbivores
That can cause such destruction.
They could destroy our home
Bring it all down around us.
Our safe place
our security
turned to dust
these tiny silent
terminators.

Dream home

I want to build a new house
exactly as in my fantasy
the perfect picture
I've constructed in my mind.
High walls
in warm calming colours
painted pressed metal ceilings
wooden doors
with brass knobs
a claw-foot bath
with sparkling stainless steel taps
marble bench tops
rustic cupboards.
All fresh and new
but with an old world feel.
There is plenty of space
and everything works.
It holds in the heat
and keeps in the cool.
The garden is beautiful
lush and full of colour
all the fences stand up straight
and keep the dogs in their place.
This is the house
from my dreams
But fantasy never translates perfectly into realty
because we can't control reality.

Wedding

Park the car at the side of a dirt road
and walk
all in finery
shiny shoes with heels
hair slicked and sprayed.
Guests all trudge and totter to
the picture perfect spot.
Everybody stands
sun beating down
sweating off make-up
running mascara.
Stand, shuffle, wait
until the gift-wrapped car arrives
the party all packed in
and padded up
like wedding gifts.
All eyes on the bride
a beautiful doll
smile from ear to ear
then the march.
Tears fall with each step
along with beads of sweat.
The celebrant speaks
slow and methodical
like he is delivering a speech
that will change lives
define a generation
free a race
or end a war.

I do's.
Maybe the best man will actually loose
the golden rings
no such luck
The precious are exchanged
and then the kiss
to seal the couple's fate.

Cake Topper

On top of the cake
He and she stands
Centre stage
Under the spotlight
All eyes on her,
…and him.
White dress
Black suit
Flowers, bows and bells
It's the way it's supposed to be
Proper
Nice
Normal
Traditional
You have made it
You're a success
The ultimate winning lottery ticket
The marriage certificate.

Ode to Matrimony

Stood in dappled light
under the outstretched limbs
of a eucalyptus tree
I hold you
and you hold me.
We part our lips
and exhale our words of love
inhaling to receive.
Symbols of our promise
of eternal fidelity
are exchanged.
We are bound together.

This is Just to Say

You have self-indulged
again
forgotten that you
are not the only one
who lives here
likes plums
needs fruit for school
and snacks for grazing
I am glad you enjoyed them
but I hope
they give you a bellyache.

The Extension

A new dwelling
was built on to an existing structure
tacked on
forced to cohabit
two separate entities
overlapping
trying to pretend
they belong to each other.
Floorboards creak
hinges groan
doors swell in the damp season.
The old features
show their distaste
for the new
through their harsh contradiction.
But the intruder
the invasion
this foreign body
is just trying to settle in
and make itself at home.

The Erosion

The kiss
a secret secured
firmly in place
when lips were locked.
The secret,
covered with lies
those lies ate away the trust
once uncovered.
Broken shire
broken home
broken heart
A girl from work? Yes? No?
Would you like to go out for a bite to eat?
Could I spend the rest of my life with her?
Lies, betrayal and secrets
the acid eating away everything it touched.

The Jar

You gave me a jar
and you filled it
with IOUs
small strips of curled paper
stating debts,
debts you cannot repay,
won't even attempt to.
You gave me a jar
and you filled it
with broken promises
the broken pieces
and remnants
of the things I'd loved
things I'd hoped for
and pieces of my dreams.
You gave me a jar
and filled it with lies
about love
about the past
the present and the future
words that you tainted
statements that were hollow.
You gave me a jar
an empty jar.

Goodbye Black Dog

She brought you into this world
and then she led you out of it.
An irreplaceable gift
turned into an unnecessary sacrifice.
You entered my life
and made an impact
I never expected.
You softened my heart.
You loved every minute of your short life
your absence will be felt
your presence will be missed
and you will never be forgotten.

Franz Marc

Franz Marc, you arrived on the 14th day of April.
You landed on the laundry floor.
Your mother a gypsy.
Your father a German.
Franz Marc, when you arrived
you entered this world backwards
with your eyes shut
and your ears closed.
Franz Marc, when you are grown
you will sit by my side
when I am lonely and low
and give me your strength.
Franz Marc, when you are grown
you will shake my hand
and walk along side of me
and experience the world.
Franz Marc, until then
you can chew my shoes
and bite my ears
but you will always have my heart.

Disappointment Man

Continual broken promises
And unfulfilled requests.
You are never
Where you say you'll be
You are never
There when it counts
You let us flounder
You let us drown.
Not a rock
Nor a haven.
You cause sadness
Pain
And instability.
In times of greatest need
We cannot trust
We cannot depend
We cannot rely
All we can depend, rely and trust to get from you
Is disappointment…

Big Men

Empty, wasted words
pointless bravado
an imaginary facade,
shallow men with hard hearts
tainted minds and dark and dirty souls.
Who are you trying to impress?
What are you trying to prove?
That you are a bigger fake than them
have a narrower mind
a colder heart
or are you just trying to prove
that you too have an absence of soul?
Those things don't make you a big man…
A true man
is gentle of heart.
A true man
is open of mind
and he knows that there is always much more to learn.
A true man
is true to his word
does not waste them
says only what needs to be said
to comfort others.
A true man
is a present father
and sees his children not only as extensions of himself
but as his future
and the future of humankind.

A true man
loves his family
above all else
always puts them first
and finds the greatest pleasure
in sitting back and quietly watching
them grow, develop and succeed
but if they need him
he is always there.
It is always all for them.

Checking In

Hello, my old friend
so we meet again
you have reappeared
to confront me
with myself
hold up a mirror
for me to take
a harsh look
at myself
and my progress
since we were last together.
I have been
moving forward
but as always
when we catch up
for these little accountability sessions
I am never where I thought I'd be
but I guess life works that way.

The End of the Love Affair I Had With the Thought of You

I am ending this
the one-sided love affair.
You tempt me
and tease
but we could never really be together
because you would be the death of me.
I toyed with the idea
fantasised and daydreamed
but every time
I made that definitive step
towards consummating our relationship
you disappeared
I'd reach out to embrace you
and it was like I had kissed death.
I no longer want you
or even to entertain
the thought of you.
You are toxic
a poison
a drug
that I was temporarily addicted too
but there was never anything more
between us
than my imagination romanticising
about us becoming one.
I was in love with the thought of you
but I am ending the affair now.

Attention Seeking

Tell me I'm pretty
tell me I'm funny
that I am smart.
Give me your full
and undivided attention
forget about the rest.
I need to know
that I can hold your concentration
that I amuse and entertain you.
I want you
to feel addicted to me
like you want to consume me
take me in with your eyes.
Breath me in
to fill your lungs.
You want to touch me
take hold and never let go.
Listen to all my words
and picture them
floating around you
keeping you safe.
Please
tell me
I'm all you need.

Brief Encounter

Slide your fingers up
into my hair
grab it
and pull gently
so my head tilts back.
Kiss my partly open mouth
and slip the tip of you tongue in
and tease me
until I bite your bottom lip.
I want you to rip off my clothes
bury your face in my neck
and breathe me in
like you are trying to absorb me.
Let's hover here
float in the pure ecstasy
of passion and wanting
before we merge
in full physical action
and it is all over
and this moment
of sweet connection
is gone.

Grief and Loss

You are not dead.
You did not leave
well not in any physical sense
I still see you
every other day
I still see you
in my daughter's eyes
but the feeling of loss
over the change
in the nature of our relationship
has bound me.
My home
my family
my security
has all fallen
down around me
and I feel exposed
left bare
and vulnerable.
An end
into emptiness?
Or a slate cleaned
for a new beginning?

Shadow Play

A whimsical cloud
floats around my head
while the mouths make shapes
shapes of lust and desire
shapes of validation
affection and flattery
I crawl in when I am weak
lonely and desperate
I wallow in the muck
rummaging through the filth
and the scum
with the other lost souls
bumping heads
and writhing on top of each other.
I physically crave the contact
with the creatures of the shadows
I am repulsed by them
but want them
all in the same instance.

Discourse

I am great
I am unaffected
I am happy
You are a liar
You are selfish
You are irritating
I am moving on
I know I need better
I know I deserve respect
You are a bitch
You are a princess
You have nothing without me
I am onto that
I am organised
I am honest
You are unproductive
You procrastinate
You exaggerate
I am building self-esteem
I am working on self-acceptance
I am clearing out the old bad habits
You don't build anything
You don't work
You should get a real job and start making money,
Everything I need
I have within
and that is enough.

Sylvia

Her story
starts beautifully
just as I hope
my story will become.
Her story is my envy
my desire.
I would be her.
I imagine I am her
but a lesser
cheaper version
a factory second.
Oh how I love her
and all she represents.
She is my idea of glamour
even to the chilling end.
I would give
almost anything
to be her
reach her achievements
her legacy
posthumous
or not to
posthumous?
That is my question.
Even her suicide
seems glamorous to me.

But it is her son
his story
that stops my fantasy
my romanticising
it awakens me
drags me
back into the world of the living.

Runaway Idea

You drew me in
with a picture
you painted with words.
I took those words
and created a fantasy.
My life
as a romantic movie
scenes of sweetness
scenes of laughter
scenes of intimacy
and excitement.
The notion I created
from the stories that you told me
had me hooked
to daydreams
and speculations
of what could be
but my wanting
lusting and desire
was all based
on an abstract perception of you
I had created
in my mind
which reality can never compete with.

Dusted with Icing Sugar

A light, fluffy
golden sponge cake
with a centre
full
of whipped cream
and strawberry jam.
Icing sugar has been sprinkled
over the top
like snow covering rooftops.
The cake is sweet
the cake is comforting
the cake is familiar
but it is just a sponge cake
made up of
a few
everyday ingredients
but when dressed up
with the jam
and the cream
and dusted with icing sugar
it makes the simple
and ordinary
sponge cake
taste much sweeter
and much more palatable.

Is This Love?

Confusion,
heaviness in my heart
someone is pushing against it.
I have swallowed a stone
and it is sat
in the pit of my stomach.
Is this love?
Should love make me feel so sick?
Am I confusing love for habit?
I feel isolated
and alone
in this 'love'
I have been dropped
into a rubber dinghy
in the middle of the ocean
the ocean is unstable
unpredictable.
Nothing feels solid
safe
or secure.
Is it just me?
Have I created this nightmare
in my own mind?
Or is the situation the cause?

The Train

Everybody climbs on
squeezes in
like sardines in a can
all wedged side by side.
The doors slide closed
the train lurches forward
everybody swings
side to side
all travelling somewhere
and although each persons destination
may be different
they are all in it together.
Connected through love, caring and compassion
protection and acceptance
we are all family
we are all lInked
each individual carriages
but joined together
to a driving force
that keeps us moving
keeps the train on track
to take us to our destination.

Heart Forms

Under extreme heat
and pressure
my heart formed
like a gemstone.
Over time layer upon layer
built in circles
my heart orbs grew.
The fault lines
and cavities
show the changes in conditions
my heart has experienced
in its lifetime.
The rings of my heart
represent the years
I have loved
The colour represents the nature
The fractures
are for those who I have lost
and the hollows
are my hidden desires.
My crystal heart
is strong and restorative
but delicate and fragile
so please don't break it.

The World

The universal family
is the continual
circle that feeds
into and on itself
forever spinning
forever rotating
heart and emotion
creativity and physicality
thoughts and worry
where we find comfort
where we find home.
Although each family looks different
and is constructed differently
they are all held together
by the same elements.

www.ingramcontent.com/pod-product-compliance
Lightning Source LLC
Chambersburg PA
CBHW062143100526
44589CB00014B/1671